BE GENTLE WITH YOUR MIND:Proven Ways to Eliminate self doubt and Negative Thinking

INTRODUCTION

Suppose you got up earlier today with a positive insight and began your day with an optimistic outlook. As you leave for work ready to go, you are thinking there isn't anything on the planet that can stop you today. You pass through the traffic and right whenever you have the opportunity to push ahead there comes a stop light. Fail.. forget about it, it's only one stoplight. Following this came another couple of stop lights. You're late for your 11 am meeting and miss your standard parking space by a couple of moments. You advise yourself that you're relentless and keep at it. Leap to 11:15, your manager has begun the gathering show without you and you're feeling everyone's eyes on you with your late section. In a split second there is only one feeling that you can feel - devastating deadness. It takes all of 60 seconds for your brilliant and happy self to enter a deep, dark hole of reasoning and a variety of considerations - what is everybody considering of me, what could be the results, do I disregard that advancement, for what reason does this happen to me? What you've recently experienced through this story is the twisting of overthinking.

Overthinking is the specialty of making issues that don't exist. Though, reflection will assist you with pushing forward with goal and reason. Overthinking pushes us to harp on wordy occasions that we might have zero command over, causing us to feel self crushed and trapped previously.

Table of content

*View Setbacks as Temporary Events

*Don't Take Failure Personally

*Put Things Into Perspective

*Remain Calm and Objective

*Keep a Gratitude Journal

*Focus on Your Accomplishments

*Give Yourself Personal Time

*Surround Yourself With Positive People

*Remove Negative Influences

*Doubt Your Doubts Before You Doubt Yourself

*Find Solutions

*Forgive Yourself

*Adopt a Healthy Lifestyle

*Serve Others

*Ask Why This Is Happening for You, Not to You

*Focus on What You Can Control

*Laugh

You Can Become More Optimistic

Chapter 1: Self reflection as opposed to Overthinking. Which one are you doing?

One of the goals of self-reflection is to look at a particular situation that we feel is unresolved so that we can understand which aspects we can control and which aspects we cannot. And then think about how you will do it differently in the future. A big part of the self-reflection process is finding a workable way to solve the problem. But that's rarely easy.

Sometimes, when we intentionally brush past an unresolved or uncomfortable situation, our self-reflection can turn into rumination, a cycle of negative and unproductive thinking that can be difficult to break. This is also known as obsessive thinking. Pondering can take the form of "Why did this happen to me?", "What if?" or aggressively blaming themselves.

Knowing this in advance can help us set expectations of ourselves. What we really want is to rewind situations to think about them... and work to resolve them without getting caught up in an overly negative thought process.

While self-reflection can be difficult, there are very positive mental health benefits to come from the process. Specifically, the self-learning curiosity and building resilience that comes with taking control of how we think about things.One study focused on the link between rumination, rumination, and depression. Self-reflective people sometimes ruminated when they couldn't find a solution to their problems, and found that rumination was related to depression while rumination was not.

Self-reflection is important to our growth, but we shouldn't force ourselves to self-reflect when we're too upset to find productive solutions. When we think about ourselves, we have to try not to be too hard on ourselves; Even when it seems overwhelming, finding a small realistic step toward resolving the situation turns thought into action

Overthinking is the specialty of making issues that don't exist. Though, reflection will assist you with pushing forward with goal and reason. Overthinking pushes us to harp on wordy occasions that we might have zero command over, causing us to feel self crushed and trapped previously.
Our minds are astonishing processors that settle on cognizant and subliminal choices as many as 35,000

times each day. Cautious examination and investigation can work on certain decisions.In any case, when is your curious nature supportive and when does overthinking really become an issue? Also, is there truly anything you can do to stop it?

How can you say whether you're overthinking? The primary thing to acknowledge about overthinking is that it can feel a huge amount like critical thinking. Yet, the two are certainly unmistakable.

Critical thinking is the point at which you pose inquiries with the goal of tracking down a response as well as instituting an answer,Overthinking, then again, is the point at which you harp on potential outcomes and entanglements with no genuine purpose of tackling an issue. Truth be told,those issues or potential issues may not actually really exist.

Overthinking can likewise now and again feel like self-reflection. Once more, the two are unmistakable.

"Self-reflection is an inside curious cycle established for a higher reason — whether that is to develop personally or gain another viewpoint. In the event that you're fixating on something you could do without about yourself that you either can't change or have zero desire to improve, it's not self-reflection — it's overthinking

In any case, at the time, overthinking can be difficult to recognize.

Signs that you may be overthinking include:

Harping on previous occasions or circumstances
Re-thinking choices you've made
Replaying your missteps in your psyche
Reiterating testing or awkward discussions
Focusing on things you have no control over, change or move along
Envisioning the worst situation imaginable or result
Following your concerns out of the current second and into an unchangeable past or unforeseeable future
"Running your rundown" while attempting to nod off
Addressing yet never settling on a choice or making a move

Chapter 2:How does overthinking influence you?

While it might feel like overthinking is simply something that occurs in your mind, it's more than that.

"Overthinking can influence how you experience and connect with your general surroundings — keeping you from pursuing significant choices, holding you back from partaking in the current second and depleting you of the energy you want to deal with everyday stressors,

Furthermore, whether you're focusing on the past or catastrophizing about what was to come, thought designs that are more horrendous than valuable can negatively affect both your emotional wellness and actual wellbeing.
From an emotional wellness point of view, nervousness can influence your capacity to adapt to regular stressors, and sadness brings about misery

Knowing how anxiety affects the body is the first step in treating and managing the symptoms and related complications that can develop.

More than 40 million[1] U.S. adults are affected by anxiety each year, and there is a growing prevalence among younger generations. Therefore, it's more important than ever to be properly informed about anxiety, so that you're better equipped to deal with it.

Have you considered clinical trials for Anxiety? We make it easy for you to participate in a clinical trial for Anxiety, and get access to the latest treatments not yet widely available - and be a part of finding a cure.

Symptoms of an anxiety disorder
Anxiety disorders can cause an array of symptoms, from mental and emotional to physical. Since signs and severity vary from person to person, they can often be misdiagnosed as another condition or cause.

How anxiety affects the mind/brain:

Increased stress hormones in the brain, which can result in feelings of nervousness, anxiousness, and agitation

Inability to reason rationally

Hold onto negative thoughts and memories

Sense of impending doom or danger

Constant worrying

Difficulty focusing.

How anxiety affects the body[2]:

Chronic exhaustion

Increased heart rate or heart palpitations
Shortness of breath
Difficulty getting sleep

Poor immunity

Aching muscles

Nausea
Shaking
Low sex drive[3]

How can you know your physical symptoms are
caused by anxiety?
It's common for a person suffering from anxiety
to become so anxious that they don't realize the
physical symptoms they're experiencing are a
result of their anxiety. In times of immense
distress, new physical symptoms can appear,
causing someone with anxiety to become more
stressed as they try to figure out whether the
symptoms are caused by anxiety or another
condition.

There are some quick and easy steps you can
take to identify whether physical symptoms are
caused by anxiety while reducing the severity of
the symptoms in the process.

Harvard Medical School[4] reports that the following steps have been shown to help identify anxiety-related physical symptoms:

Stop and assess

Distract yourself

Relax your body or work it

Reassure yourself

The first step is to take a step back and assess the situation. Observe what is happening to your body, how it relates to your emotional state and the possibility that it is in response to an intense period of stress.

After assessing your situation and symptoms, distracting yourself from focusing on the symptoms can help ease their impact. Common practices include house chores, reading a book/magazine, watching funny videos, and running errands around town.

Another step in the right direction is doing a light exercise like running or a more calming routine like yoga and meditation to relax your body. Participating in physical activities can lighten the stress and tension you're experiencing.

When you become more aware of the possibility that anxiety is causing your symptoms, reassuring yourself that what you're experiencing isn't as terrifying as it seems can be helpful. Remind yourself that these symptoms will pass.

If these steps don't improve your quality of life when physical symptoms occur, consult your doctor for more insight into the cause.

Find more techniques to calm your anxiety and identify its causes here.

Conditions that can result from having an anxiety disorder
Studies show that people diagnosed with common anxiety disorders like social anxiety, phobias, panic disorder, and generalized anxiety disorder have a higher association with certain medical conditions.

For instance, a 2015 study[5] published in the Journal of Psychosomatic Research reported that patients with anxiety and depression symptoms are more likely to experience additional conditions such as:

Heart disease

Back pain

Ulcers

Declining eyesight

Asthma

Migraines headaches

In the study, patients diagnosed with anxiety disorder were interviewed and evaluated on the severity of anxiety and depressive symptoms they experienced and associated medical conditions. The study found that as the severity of anxiety and depressive symptoms increased, so did the odds of developing one or more of these conditions.

An additional study conducted in 2017[6] confirmed these findings in the elderly population, adding that anxiety was associated with heart disease, depression was associated with asthma, and a combination of anxiety and depression contributed to persistent cough, asthma, hypertension, heart disease, vision problems, and gastrointestinal problems.

Tips for managing and treating the physical symptoms of anxiety
One of the biggest misconceptions about anxiety is that it's 'all in your head'. In fact, anxiety is a

very real and serious medical condition that requires regular management and treatment. When left untreated, anxiety can lead to more serious conditions that could have otherwise been reduced or prevented.

Common treatments for anxiety include psychotherapy like cognitive behavioral therapy (CBT), and exposure therapy.

CBT is helpful for identifying the thoughts and actions that lead to damaging feelings so that you can work towards changing them.

Exposure therapy is a mixture of imagery, activities, and exercises focused on confronting and overcoming fears.

Other treatment options include prescription antidepressants to improve mood and decrease stress, beta-blockers to reduce physical symptoms like rapid heartbeat, and anti-anxiety medication (benzodiazepines) to relieve panic and worry symptoms[7]. Medication options and mixtures vary from person to person and should be discussed with your doctor to find the right fit.

What You Need to Know About Your Anxiety Medication

Self-care can be helpful in managing symptoms as well. The most beneficial practices include calming techniques, getting enough sleep, being physically active, and avoiding nicotine, alcohol, and caffeine.

See our complete guide to treating anxiety here.

The lowdown

When experiencing new or reoccurring physical symptoms, remember:

Anxiety affects the body in many mental, emotional, and physical ways.

Take a moment to assess and observe your symptoms to identify the cause behind them.

Practice self-care in your daily routines and consult a doctor about medication or psychotherapy treatments if your quality of life declines.

Treat and manage your anxiety-related symptoms to prevent additional conditions from emerging as a result.
At the point when it's an opportunity to tackle something, set a cutoff time for pursuing your last choice. Greater choices will call for greater investment, so consider enjoying reprieves to occupy yourself when or on the other hand if the dynamic cycle becomes overpowering.

Make a move on the things you have some control over and let go of the things you can't When you notice you're "in your mind" about something, inquire as to whether your contemplations can be made more valuable — towards going with a choice or tracking down an answer.

In the event that your thinking design can't be made more productive, you're probably harping on something beyond your control — whether that is on the grounds that it's now worked out, might in all likelihood never occur or essentially can't be changed. Be careful with these negative contemplations and consider making progress toward letting them go.

One method for relinquishing the unsolvable is to see these as 'gravity issues.' We have zero control over or change a few features of life, similarly as we can't fix gravity. We may, in any case, work on the perspectives that we can change all things being equal,

.

Chapter3:How to manage Anxiety and Relieve stress

Your mind is the control room of the body, this implies your cerebrum controls everything, including the body, its capabilities, how you feel and think. Via preparing your cerebrum, you can learn methods and rules that will empower you to defeat the fundamental reason for misery and nervousness.

Uneasiness, basically, is a high level of stress. Stress has developed into a consistent, most pessimistic scenario, situations and uncertainties turning round the cerebrum with unrelenting irritation, questions, and fears which radically drains your profound energy, sending your tension level taking off. Your uneasiness, thus, impedes your regular routine, objectives, and connections.

The uplifting news is that this constant propensity can be broken, and in this article you'll investigate ways you can prepare your cerebrum to battle tension, remain composed and see life from a more uplifting outlook. In any case, to do this, you should understand a couple of things. Allow me to take you through the excursion of preparing your mind to battle uneasiness.

Mindfulness"Your center decides your world."

Know
Ponder your thought process
Arrange/Catalog
Assign
The most vital phase in fighting nervousness contains an alternate concentration. Know about your viewpoints. Ponder your thought process and don't allow your considerations to control you any longer. Control your contemplations. To hold things under wraps, you could begin a journal if you can. Carry out a means of classifying your contemplations. On the off

chance that one of those totally regrettable considerations comes into your psyche, list it and assign it as bad, one you ought not be enjoyed.It is a very interesting question. Our parts are born with us and end with us, The same is the case with the mind. JOHN MILTON's famous line:" It's the mind that makes a heaven of hell or a hell of heaven." "US" is the area of man's life in this world : his ambition, attempts, his success, his fall, his perseverance -comprising the whole gamut of life. The mind is born to control man and his actions. This control is in the realm of the- day- to day life of man. Its influence on his life is very important. Certain things are acceptable in life. If the mind encourages these, allow the mind its way. But certain, are not. So the mind needs a control over it. If the mind encourages the socially accepted good things then it can be allowed to control us. If it encourages anti-social tendencies, then it has to be bridled and controlled. Man allows the mind to control his actions if he is not clear about the direction of his life! If he is, he wants to control his mind. The desire to control the mind comes as we move up the ladder of life! We have to achieve something in life. The mind has to be controlled and directed along our path of life. Hatred, envy, kama, krodha, lobha, matha, marcharya - these are the detractors and destroyers of life! To get rid of these qualities, the MIND has to be controlled. That is what the sages and seers have done to deliver a lot of good to mankind! To get complete control over the mind is the ultimate success in life.

While doing this, remember that overcoming your contemplations isn't simply a game that can be played when you feel like it. It is a responsibility forever, this implies, when you start you can't stand to stop. Things we do is what we decided to do so, as being on the high school years i've learn the lesson of "Mind and actions" as we think things and decide to do it as we probably thinks of an act and decide to do the act

A similar orthodoxy long dominated neuropsychology: the brain controls the mind, which has no independent existence outside of the chemical reactions and patterns which constantly fire inside our brains. Neuro-biologists have long held that the brain exclusively drives the mind, and that the mind serves only the individual self.

But a new breed of medical scientists is challenging this linear approach to the relationship between the objective physical world and subjective mental life ,it is a collection of thoughts, patterns, perceptions, beliefs, memories and attitudes. "The mind can use the brain to perceive itself, and the mind can be used to change the brain."

Which investigates how cultural and social relations inform brain development, how the brain organizes such experiences and knowledge, and how such developments in turn give rise to a cultural brain.

Our cultural practices such as emotional bonds to family or religious devotion are themselves repetitive patterns of energy use that stimulate (from the outside) discernable neural firing patterns and synaptic connections.

Our brains become used to, and even develop a preference for, certain patterns, meaning the brain can be trained to behave, and even gradually evolve, based on the activities of the mind.

Technology is helping us shed ever more focused light on which parts of our brain direct specific actions or respond to diverse stimuli,and advancements in artificial intelligence have benefited from such insights,leading to devices which can "read your mind," discern signals of will and intention, for example with respect to where you wish to move a computer mouse, and translate that intent into action. By this logic, culture is literally a "state of mind," a cluster of signals which believers of a certain faith share in common ,by extension, cultural evolution is to some extent the mutation of patterns of mental signals shared by groups of people.

Dole out a time frame to worry

One of the definitive methods for controlling tension is through delay, and this is the most effective way to accomplish it.

It's exceedingly difficult to be useful in anything you're doing when tension is gobbling up a major lump of your viewpoints. Getting yourself diverted or advising yourself to stop the concern doesn't actually finish the work - basically not for a really long time.

So what should be possible about this?

Here is the trick!

As opposed to attempting to dispose of these concerns, award yourself the authorization to have it, yet delay it until some other time.

The most vital phase in fighting tension utilizing this approach is to make a chance to stress. Most likely the overall setting ought to be between

5:00 to 5:30 pm and in the solace of your room, simply ensure the time span is a piece early, so it won't make you restless just before you head to bed.

The following stage to have as a primary concern is the deferment interaction, when it's not yet time, in the event that a fear jumps into your head, you can make a rundown of it and afterward go on about your day. Remembering that you have opportunity and willpower to consider it later, so there's a positively compelling reason to get all restless or stressed over it at the present time.

During your concern period - It's currently time to set the straightforward, go over your rundown and permit yourself to stress over any and everything likewise having a severe rule for the time span. Also, whenever you don't have anything, or you're shy of things to stress over, cheerfully avoid the period and partake in the remainder of your day.

This has been one of the best approaches to ending the propensity for stress or harping on genuine fears as opposed to having a useful day obviously. Since there's no longing of stifling and totally combating nervousness, you gradually get to have outright command over the circumstance.

Stress/Problem Solving

Indeed, these are totally two unique things, and despite the fact that critical thinking includes assessing what is happening, it doesn't harp on it. While attempting to find an answer, you initially think of substantial advances and afterward set those means in motion.

On the off chance that a genuine fear swims into your head, do well to find out if you can really think of an answer for it. Stressing rarely brings answers, regardless of how long you think about it.

But, let's be clear and honest…

After 10+ years of regular meditation and after secluding myself for years doing only meditation, almost all day (I was actually a monk)… I still have problems in my life, like all humans on this planet.

So meditation (alone) doesn't solve problems.

Problems are challenging us to solve them. Actually they are what makes us become better human beings. So we should learn to love them and face them.

There are some problems that just need a little time to get sorted… And meditation can help in clarifying the situation.

About the "big life problems" you are talking about, the only way I know to solve them are proper actions, done with a clear mind for the right period of time, with a good intention.

These big problems that affect our lives are mostly coming from behavior, thinking patterns, beliefs, conditionings, characters we built up over time coming from our background, family or impressions of our childhood...

Meditation helps to become aware of all this and to not act automatically on this stuff, but learn to observe these patterns in ourselves and decide to learn from them. Use them instead of being used!

And only by knowing our patterns can we plan the proper actions to build new more empowering beliefs and conditionings.

Every time we define a situation as a "problem" it means that somewhere there is a solution to that problem. Otherwise we wouldn't call it a problem... Right?

There is not a big problem or a little problem...
A problem it's a problem... Big or little it's just a
point of view!

For example, Try to remember a little problem
you had when you were a child... it was
bothering you so much... Now how does it
look?

What is different in solving my problems after I
started to meditate regularly is the way I face my
problems and find multiple solutions.

Problems always look much bigger than they
are. True or true!? Do you remember the
problems we had when we were children? It
looked so big...

I believe that problems never show to someone
that doesn't have the ability to face them and
learn and grow stronger from them! A little child
has little responsibility and little problems...

The biggest source of problems in our life is that we don't feel we have the energy or the knowledge to solve our problems...

It's a matter of fact, how can you effectively face a problem if your energy is below zero?

Sometimes we feel that problems are so overwhelming that it feels so hard to find a solution and we start to think there is no solution...

And what we think we start to see in our life, our selective attention starts to see around confirmation validating our thoughts...

And we feel stuck. But there is always a solution, always.

So, to wrap it up.

Meditation can help you solve your life problems, elevate your energy, giving you more focus and clarity of mind but... Meditation it's not enough. You need to act, and face your problems.

Maybe little by little, but you need to face them!

Take responsibility for your energy and your daily meditation!

You have all my sympathy and blessings

While managing stress, attempt to distinguish in the event that there's an answer or not, and on the off chance that there's an answer, you can make a move immediately as opposed to considering and harping on them.

Figure out how to acknowledge your sentiments, own your concerns, and you'll be in charge of the circumstance.

challenge your thoughts and anxiety.

Do not hold on to anger or any negative emotions. They tend to simmer in your brain and fester and slowly poison you from within. You don't know anything is wrong until you suddenly realize your heart has become clouded with doubt, lack of self confidence, anger, frustration, paranoia, anxiety.

Openly talk about what's bothering you. Doesn't have to be with someone, can be just you alone. And in your talks be brutally honest with yourself. Talk openly about your failings, frustrations, achievements, dreams, aspirations. Get that negative energy out of your thoughts and out in the open where it can't harm you. You'll feel better for it.

Understand a person driven by your emotions or archetypes as Carl Jung described them. Understanding these emotions, appetites, inclinations and how they rule us is a lifelong process. Mastering them is your aim. This is slow painful work because it requires a lot of honest introspection. It also requires an open mind and the ability to step out of your comfort zone and challenge your assumptions. But if you're able to, you will be a much happier person. A person who chooses how to react to situations and whatever life throws at you instead of being a vehicle or mouthpiece for his emotions and appetites

Persistent negative thinking contributes to anxiety and may lead to feelings of low mood. Some ways to manage negative thinking are:

Understand your thinking pattern. This can be a preliminary step in initiating a change. Identify your chain of thoughts and notice if you look at things through a 'black' or 'white' lens, considering only the extremes.

Stay away from stopping your thoughts. The more we try to stop our thoughts, the more they tend to come up and lead to unsettling feelings. Let your thoughts flow in an organic way, distancing yourself in the process.

Try to label your thoughts. Take a step back and label your thoughts. The intention here is not to change or avoid your thoughts. Notice these thoughts and let them flow.

Challenge your negative assumptions. A lot of times, our assumptions tend to cause restlessness. Seek evidence for or against your thoughts and this can help you channelise your energy in the present while also replacing irrational thoughts with more rational ones.

Anxiety and depression are two very different disorders, though they can co-exist.

Anxiety disorder is a sense of discomfort or fear in your own skin, it comes excessively and irrationally at times. Small problems become huge problems. It's like you want to claw out of your body in any situation that brings you even the slightest uneasiness. Think of it like a huge brick wall beginning to form around you when you want to see what's in front. You try to break it down with a hammer, you may even ask others to join and help you, but no one else notices this wall. It's that creeping feeling of worry and paranoia like you clearly know the wall doesn't exist, but it's still there; everything is out of your control yet simultaneously all in your head, except you feel that all the time.

A depressive disorder is a baseline negative mood, constant sadness, detachment of reality and general disinterest in life. People who are depressed seem to find "normal" activities, such as getting out of bed and small social interaction, to be a challenge. They lack the motivation to be productive in any way and lose all passion for things they once enjoyed. Sometimes, suicidal thoughts and active pursuit to take their own life comes as a result of depression. However, rather than making an effort to die, it is commonly found that most depressed people wish they simply never existed. Think of it like having a bunch of toys you loved to play with, that once gave you the best experiences. Gradually, the toys begin to seem dull and you can't imagine why you ever liked playing with them. You had a big blue rocketship with a dinosaur named Leroy inside that would shoot up into space to destroy meteors. Now, it just seems like a bunch of plastic pieces you hold in the air and make stupid sound effects with. Boring. Unfulfilling. A meaningless fog hovering around you which should eventually fade away but it doesn't, except you feel that all the time.

Anxiety and depression exist separately, but they often hold hands, like two best friends. Anxiety is caring too much and depression is not caring enough.

Testing intolerance of Uncertainty

You need to acknowledge the way that pondering the future and stressing over it doesn't actually transform it. Attempting to control the future, since you anticipated that things are going to turn out badly is unimaginable. You can't change the result by stressing over it.

Quit getting stressed over vulnerabilities for this is the way to nervousness alleviation.

I'll give you 5 habits that cause low self-esteem which by default bring one into a depressive state along with 5 habits that create self-esteem. This way, you can choose which habits you'd like to create or abandon.

Creators of LOW self-esteem:

Compare your "inside" life (how you feel) to everyone else's "outside" (what you see/believe) life.
Place your self-worth, value, self-confidence, "self", in other people's hands.

Wallow in self-pity. Have a daily pity party for you and yourself where you relive all the shitty moments of your life, retell all the sad stories and talk about all the missed opportunities and mistakes you made.
Focus on the fact that nobody calls you, checks up on you, cares about you when they know you're in a "bad" place.
Keep thinking about how fucked your life really is. How EVERYONE has it better than you, easier than you, more than you, and if THEY only knew… blah blah blah.
Creators of HIGH self-esteem.

Focus only on your assets. List them. Every day, add to the list. When you wake, dress, drive, walk, work, smile, talk - make sure you and your assets are the only things representing you.
This is your life. There are no do-overs. Stop living this life for other people. Those voices. The ones saying. "You shouldn't, can't, you're not good enough, this enough, that enough etc." None of those voices belong to you. Tell them to shut the hell up! They had their chance to live

their life. Don't let them force their bad choices on you. You decide what you want, like, don't like, value, treasure, believe, etc.

The past. It's your greatest asset. Learn from it. Find the lessons. Every painful experience is an opportunity for growth and an opportunity to help someone else through the same experience. Stop feeling sorry for your sorry ass.

The way to build self-esteem is to do esteemable actions. Help others. Take the focus off of you, yourself and your pity and place it on helping other people. Period. Smile. Open doors. Let the other driver in. Buy a cup of coffee for a stranger. Call someone and ask how THEY are doing. DO NOT expect a thank you, and DO NOT talk about yourself.

Whatever you focus on magnifies. If you want to find what's shitty about something, you'll find it. If you want to find what's great, you'll find it too. It's about wanting the things that you already have. When you do...you'll get more and more of what you want.

When you smile at the world. Guess what, the world smiles back. The best way to get a hug if you want one…is to give one.

Having low self-esteem is… being bullied as a child and being totally perplexed as to what you're doing wrong to deserve this. It's watching your friends leave to join the bullies because it's more fun than being on the receiving end. You have now learned that people will be embarrassed to be associated with you and will leave when they learn who you are. All friendships will hurt you eventually; why set yourself up for that? Worse still, before age 10, you're sure death would be a welcome opportunity.

Having low self-esteem is… knowing (you don't just think so, you're sure it's fact) that no one wants to be around you because, at best, you're a disappointing experience to others, hoping to fade away and go unnoticed to avoid further embarrassing yourself and, at worst, you ARE noticed, to your detriment. People don't just look through you, they look AT you and you can't avoid their gaze and the subsequent judgment. It then becomes an easy decision to avoid people since it's all downside.

Having low self-esteem is… doing objectively well at school, but requesting you stop receiving consolatory praise from family. They're only saying that because they're family and they love you. There are two outcomes: 1) you do what you are supposed to do, which is perform perfectly or 2) you fail to perform perfectly. You're not "excelling" or "succeeding," you're performing as expected.

Having low self-esteem is… not even considering a romantic relationship because people don't even want to be associated with you, let alone be friends. And then to further expect that they find anything about you attractive?? You can't even fantasize because it's just such a ridiculous notion!

When your friend in junior high school basically has to wear you down to take her to the prom and, when asked to dance, you hide in a phone booth in the hotel, eventually calling your parents, while her friends try to coax you out. When in high school, you receive a 3-page handwritten letter from a friend indicating her romantic feelings for you, but that she is not one to "make the first move," so essentially, she'll be waiting for an answer, which never comes, while you continue to smile and be friends like it never happened.

A year later in high school, another friend discusses the idea that neither of you have ever kissed anyone and she'd be embarrassed to go to college under such circumstances. After much polite refusal, your father has to beg and eventually flat-out pay you per date. Some time goes by and you feel unsettling mixed feelings of physical enjoyment with mental discomfort coupled with a serious GI condition that worsens with anxiety. You eventually break up with her because her entire basis for this "relationship" feels empty and practical. She was going to

leave you after high school months later anyway
(not a presumption).

You decide relationships are just eventual
disappointment and everyone will leave you as
they always have. Best not invest any mental and
emotional energy even entertaining the idea.

Having low self-esteem is… pursuing actuarial
science as a profession in college specifically
because it requires passing exams for guaranteed
job advancement instead of having to exhibit
initiative and confidence, neither of which you
have. And yet, with each exam taken, you're
sure you'll fail. And yet, with each exam
PASSED, you're still sure you'll fail next time.
And yet, with exams continuously passed,
you're sure you'll still be fired because of your
incompetence, some of it based in reality, some
unfounded, and the never-ending cavalcade of
"tomorrows" and "what ifs" that await you.

Having low self-esteem is… inevitably losing
your career, subsequently losing your friends
(you still didn't believe people wanted to be

around you anyway), and any subconscious hope you might've inexplicably had in a secure future. You've lost the life you've built on a foundation of stress and anxiety. The idea of dying sounds better than it ever has. But you can't even do THAT! Your fear of pain comes to the surface, your fear of failure follows. Your fear of disappointing those you'd leave behind for giving up and hurting them in that way, something you were quite sure you were doing regardless, while alive.

And so, with no job or friends or love or fun, no hope or future or confidence or desire, you realize you have failed at both life AND death, stuck here for another 50+ years of disappointment for you and from you.

Chapter 4:Embracing Positive Thoughts

In the wake of perusing this piece, I'll suggest that you start your excursion of defeating tension and gloom now. With a specialist you will see extra advantages as it will assist you with revealing hidden issues including past or adolescence injury and you see the outcomes considerably quicker.

As you begin directing and stay predictable, you will find that you are improving consistently. Before long enough the intrinsic mental abilities of your cerebrum will begin to dominate, and you will begin to perceive new, engaging ways of carrying requests to the turmoil of your brain and considerations.

Indeed, that is all there is to it. It's currently time to assume command over your viewpoints. Your life will unquestionably alter as a result of positive thought, which then inspires positive behavior.

Before I started my own business, I used to work as an electrical engineer. In order to read the news as soon as I arrived at work before the working day started, I had a habit of stopping at the neighborhood corner store every day on the way to work to pick up my daily newspaper.

Even before my day had officially started, I had already filled my head with the bad news, which made me feel down and defeated which would leave me feeling low, flattened and very pessimistic myself, as well. Retaining all of that antagonism toward the beginning of the day implied that wherever I turned and wherever I looked, that was all I could see. Exactly the way in which the world was terrible. Exactly the way that troublesome life was.

However, all of that changed in 2015 when I chose to completely change myself to improve things; fabricating an unimaginable business with my accomplice and genuinely starting to carry on with life in my own particular manner.

The most remarkable example I learned in that year was that:

Considerations transform into significance. Significance transforms into feeling. Also, feeling transforms right into it.

This turned into my mantra and I am right here, these years after the fact, appreciative to say that energy has turned into my lifestyle. I track down the positive in each situation, in each circumstance. I don't zero in on issues; I sort out arrangements. Dread no longer drives me; I'm driven by enthusiasm, inspiration and yearn for progress.

In this way, assuming you're battling with embracing energy in your own life, here are a few top tips that I carried out myself, on the most proficient method to foster a propensity for positive reasoning, which will, thusly, lead to positive activity and a genuinely certain and blissful life.

. Make A Massive Action Ecosystem

Your current circumstance - and that implies without question, all that you encircle yourself with - is so very strong. You are continually engrossing the energy from everything in your area, and on the off chance that that energy is negative, that is precisely the exact thing you're taking in as well.

Establish a climate that permits no pessimism at all. This incorporates the things you watch on TV, individuals you follow via web-based entertainment, your family and your companions - even down to the garments you wear and the music you pay attention to.

To have a positive life, you want to eliminate anything that isn't positive - so go on a binge of eliminating whatever takes steps to cut you down. What's more, on the other side, fill your existence with energy in each regard.

This is a gigantic initial step which you will feel the impacts of basically straight away yet that will endure all through your life, as long as you keep up with the upkeep of your good climate.

Get Clear On Your Goals

A significant number of us float through existence with no thought where we're really going. We don't actually have any idea what we need from life since we've never truly gotten some margin to figure everything out.

However, did you have at least some idea that the individuals who have objectives are multiple times bound to prevail than those without? This is quite possibly the most compelling motivation why getting clear on your objectives and doing some objective setting practices is so significant.

Having objectives naturally places you into a good perspective; you at last have a dream, you understand what course you're going in and you feel like you have a reason.

So carve out opportunities to get clear on your own objectives.

What is it that you need to accomplish before the year's over? Toward the following year's end? In five years time? Throughout your life? When you know, you can begin making an arrangement to arrive. Shut out the trepidation and get EXCITED. Now is the right time to make the daily routine YOU need to experience.

Become Aware Of Your Conditioning
To fix your negative reasoning propensities, it's fundamental to comprehend how you got those propensities in any case. Furthermore, a great deal of this boils down to negative molding during our childhood.

Large numbers of us have grown up with a negative disposition towards life thus a wide range of parts of it, particularly cash. Furthermore, there's nobody to fault on the grounds that any place we got those convictions, those individuals were likewise presumably exposed to a similar growing up - unwittingly giving their convictions to us.

You might imagine that cash is scant and hard to procure. That life is intense. That you're not equipped for specific things as a result of X, Y and Z. In any case, this is simply molding. Furthermore, the uplifting news is: you can RECONDITION yourself.

There is so much accessible to us these days that there is not any justification to fortify those old, poisonous conviction frameworks any longer.

Go on YouTube or Spotify and begin consuming positive substances. Learn about examples of overcoming adversity. Utilize positive insistences to change your old convictions.

You can in a real sense adjust your perspective on anything - simply be really watchful about what you change it to.

Become Aware Of Your Fear And Negative Thoughts

In any event, when you really do figure out how to embrace a more certain lifestyle, there will be times when dread and cynicism crop up. Also, that is completely fine! It simply shows you where there is more work to be finished.

At the point when this occurs, stop yourself and pause for a minute to notice these considerations and sort out why they've come up and what they're attempting to show you. When you know this, you'll have the option to disperse the apprehension, flip them on their head and transform them into additional positive considerations.

It's just about turning out to be more aware of the considerations you're thinking and figuring out how to deliver the ones that don't encourage you.

Gather Speed In Your Life
As hard as things might appear at specific times in your day to day existence and regardless of how negative you feel about everything, you can

begin rolling out an improvement by making little everyday moves towards one of your objectives (or every one of them!).

The facts really confirm that the initial step is generally the hardest, however whenever you've taken it you'll begin gathering speed and the entire universe will get behind you to push you forward. Whether you need to work on your wellness, eat strongly, begin a business, fabricate another expertise... regardless, it simply takes a responsibility from you to reliably take action.

The more you do, step by step, and the more you commend your successes en route, the more sure you will turn into. That energy has a gradually expanding influence and as the force fabricates you'll believe you should do and accomplish to an ever increasing extent, in all kinds of parts of your life.

Begin gathering speed by making a move each and every day

A test

At the point when you've been thinking adversely for what seems like forever, particularly when you haven't even known about it, it won't be a basic short-term switch where you'll get up one morning and the world will be brilliant and delightful and life will be great. Absolutely no chance.

However, you need to begin somewhere to change your old negative convictions and one thing I strongly suggest is an everyday appreciation practice. On the off chance that you awaken and begin your day with appreciation, you will watch and see as it spreads and lights up as long as you can remember.

Begin with finishing a day to day appreciation diary for 30 days where you record no less than 3 things that you're appreciative for, each and every day. This urges you to search for the positive qualities in your day to day existence and will assist you with zeroing in on more greatness as you approach your day. Thus, will really assist with bringing more goodness into your life.

This could totally completely change yourself to improve things - assuming that change is what you ridiculously care about. So would you say you are equipped in every way necessary for the situation?

At last…

Roy T. Bennet says in the Light of the Heart:

"Disposition is a decision. Satisfaction is a decision. Idealism is a decision. Graciousness is a decision. Giving is a decision. Regard is a decision. Anything that decision you make makes you. Pick admirably."

We each have a decision every single day that we are honored to be alive. We get to pick where we place our concentration.

If you have any desire to foster a propensity for positive reasoning and carry on with a positive life, center around energy and that is the very thing that you'll continuously get a greater amount of. Begin now. Begin today!

We all face challenges now and again, but it is our reaction to those challenges that determine how quickly we can overcome them.

Chapter 5: Turn Your Pessimism And Optimism

Optimistic people have better job security, are more likely to succeed in their careers, and have greater job satisfaction. They are able to turn disappointments into motivation, which leads to increased productivity and accomplishments.

Optimistic people get sick less often and recover from illnesses faster.

The true measure of "mental fitness" is how optimistic you are about yourself and your life. To become mentally fit, you need to learn how to control your thinking in very specific ways so that you feel terrific about yourself and your situation, no matter what happens.

So, here are 19 tips you can start using to help with positive thinking, overcoming challenges, and attracting success in your life.

Control Your Reactions and Responses

There are a few basic differences in the reactions of optimists and pessimists. The first difference is that the optimist sees a setback as temporary, while the pessimist sees it as permanent.

The optimist sees an unfortunate event, such as an order that falls through or a sales call that fails, as something that is limited in time, part of the process, and has no lasting impact on the future.

The pessimist, on the other hand, sees negative situations as damaging and a precursor to what is ahead in the future. They see these experiences as part of destiny.

So, when you find yourself in a difficult or disappointing situation, take a moment to really reflect on the challenge before you react. Try to visualize the next step towards improvement rather than responding to the setbacks that you have no control over.

Do not let one negative event impact the other aspects of your life and the opportunities that you face.

Isolate the Incident

Another difference between the optimist and the pessimist is that the optimist sees difficulty as a singular event, while the pessimist sees them as universal.

This means that when things go wrong for the optimist, they look at the event as an isolated incident largely disconnected from other things that are going on in their life.

A pessimist will take the incident and add it to a laundry list of other things going on in their life. They have a largely negative outlook on everything and tend to expand the stress they feel towards one issue onto other, unrelated areas of their life.

So, to remain positive, try to remind yourself that just because you are facing a setback in one area — whether that be a project at work falling behind or not hitting a milestone set — does not mean that the entire goal is obsolete. You may simply need to modify your plan.

A single setback may seem big at the moment, but in reality, you can quickly overcome most setbacks with the right outlook. Isolating the incident allows you to take the setback in stride and then move on from it.

View Setbacks as Temporary Events

For example, if something you were counting on failed to materialize and you interpreted it to yourself as being an unfortunate event but something that happens in the course of life and business, you would be reacting like an optimist.

The pessimist, on the other hand, sees disappointments as being pervasive. That is, to them they are indications of a problem or shortcoming that pervades every area of life.

If you find yourself in this situation, take a moment to remind yourself, that you are always capable of making change and nothing is set in stone. A glass half full mentality leads an optimist to believe that something better is coming, giving them something to work for.

A pessimist gives up, letting a single setback affect the other areas of their life. This can cause a negative ripple effect on your life, while the person with an optimistic outlook stays motivated in any situation and uses the power of positive thinking.

Don't Take Failure Personally

It can be extremely difficult at times to see the positive side of failure. An optimist sees events as external, while pessimists interpret events as personal.

An optimist tries not to take negative situations personally or as a reflection of their self-worth. Although failure is not something anyone wants to deal with, the optimist uses it as a learning opportunity.

If the optimist is cut off in traffic, for example, instead of getting angry or upset, they will simply downgrade the importance of the event by saying something like, "Oh, well, I guess that person is just having a bad day."

The optimist doesn't think they were cut off because that person had malicious intentions against them. The pessimist, on the other hand, has a tendency to take everything personally. If the pessimist is cut off in traffic, they will react as though the other driver has deliberately acted to upset and frustrate them.

When faced with what might feel like a failure, analyze the role you may have played in it to see what you might do differently to improve or prevent a similar situation in the future. If circumstances were out of your control, do not take it personally. Be self-aware and take responsibility for your actions and view the actions of others as external factors out of your control.

Put Things Into Perspective

Looking at the bigger picture allows you to act calmly and work through any situation as the optimist did in the above example. In fact, you can even go further and turn any negative situation into a positive one. By allowing the person to cut you off, you may have helped them get to work on time or meet a deadline.

When negative events happen, put them into perspective. See the big picture and do not get caught up in the details.

Remember that the inevitable setbacks that you face are temporary, specific, and external. View a negative situation as a single event that is not connected to other potential events and that is often caused largely by external factors over which you can have little control.

Refuse to see an event as being in any way permanent, pervasive, or indicative of personal incompetence or inability. You may not be able to control events, but you can control the way you react to them. The earlier you learn this, the happier you will be in life.

Remain Calm and Objective

When you are truly an optimist, you have the ability to be both objective and unemotional when caught up in the inevitable storms of daily life. You can continue to talk to yourself in a positive and optimistic way no matter what is happening in your life.

This allows you to keep your mind calm, clear, and completely under control despite the external circumstances. Because you are more relaxed and aware, you are much more capable of interpreting events more efficiently.

So, when an optimist is met with a challenge or area of stress, they are much better equipped to stay positive and overcome it. They are able to stay in complete control, act proactively, and not let external forces cloud their judgment.

On the other hand, a pessimist may get caught up in their emotions, leading them to get angry, upset, and distracted. This causes them to handle problems poorly, think irrationally, and make things harder than they really have to be by acting reactively instead of proactively.

If you feel overwhelmed or like your blood is boiling, practice being calm in these situations. Although easier said than done, staying calm and thinking positively can change your life.

Keep a Gratitude Journal

Making regular entries in a gratitude journal helps you focus on the positive things that are occurring in your life. Feeling grateful makes you a happier, more optimistic person.

Research studies involving people keeping gratitude journals show they are more optimistic, feel better about their lives, exercise more, and make fewer visits to a doctor.

Increase your positive thinking by making a habit of writing down three to five things you are grateful for each day. You will become more self-aware and see your perspective change so that you are focusing on the positive aspects of your life instead of dwelling on the negative or things out of your control.

Focus on Your Accomplishments

When you have important responsibilities to work and family, stress can tempt you to become overwhelmed by your long to-do list. You may reach the end of the day and wonder how you have gotten closer to your goals.

A pessimistic person tends to think more about the things they have not accomplished. They focus more on their mistakes as well.

However, an optimistic person sees the value in each incremental step made toward a goal. They stay positive, maintain their self-esteem, and focus on what they have accomplished.

So, instead of stressing over what you have not completed on your to-do list, make a mental or written list each night of the things you did accomplish. Your attitude will become more positive, which will motivate you to accomplish more instead of feeling burdened.

Give Yourself Personal Time

It is important to take a break from your daily responsibilities and duties. Overworking yourself leads to poor physical and mental health and a negative attitude, making it harder for you to be optimistic.

Schedule regular time in your week to do things that refresh you. Having quiet solitude gives you time to reflect, destress, and gain perspective.

Regular exercise improves your mood, lowers your stress level, reduces rates of depression and anxiety, and increases self-confidence. Take a daily walk, join a local sports team, or work out three to five days a week.

Devote time to a hobby, read uplifting books, or schedule time with close friends or family members. Giving yourself personal time on a regular basis leads to greater optimism and happiness.

Surround Yourself With Positive People

Positive attitudes are contagious. Identify the people in your life that you look up to for their optimism and spend more time with them.

Observe the things they say, what they do, and what they choose not to do or say. You will notice patterns that you can adopt that will help you be more positive as well.

A life coach can be a positive source of motivation. They can help you build the skills needed for greater self-confidence, self-awareness, and optimism.

Equally important is to identify people who have a negative influence on you. If you can avoid these individuals or cut off ties, do so. If you cannot, such as a coworker or family member, find ways to minimize their influence on you. You can also learn to advocate for yourself as you become more optimistic.

Remove Negative Influences

Similar to minimizing your contact with negative people, get rid of things that bring you down as well.

For many people, this can include watching the news, spending time on social media, listening to music that is not uplifting or working in a negative environment. Notice how you feel when you do these and other things that are part of your daily or weekly routine. If you feel overburdened, negative, stressed, angry, deflated, self-conscious, or any other negative emotions, that is a clue to replace these activities with positive ones.

Stay positive by filling your environment with pleasant, uplifting, and nurturing things. Decorate your home, room, or office with cheerful colors, comfortable furniture, and plants. Listen to music with positive lyrics. Fill your time with productive activities, such as being creative, helping others, and learning new skills.

Doubt Your Doubts Before You Doubt Yourself

Negative thoughts bring us down. When we entertain negative thoughts, we can convince ourselves we will fail even if there is no evidence to support it.

Pessimistic thinkers are full of doubts and unwilling to make changes or take risks that could improve their lives. Optimistic thinkers are full of hope and focus on the possibilities life can bring them.

When you have negative thoughts, fears, or doubts, challenge those thoughts by asking yourself why you are having them. Are they based on any real evidence?

If not, turn the thought into a positive one. Ask yourself "what if" something positive happened instead of negative and make that your thought process instead.

An excellent way to maintain a more positive outlook is to read motivational quotes daily. Subscribe to social media channels that provide daily uplifting content, read motivational books, listen to motivational podcasts, or get a calendar or planner that includes motivational quotes to cultivate optimism.

Find Solutions

Every problem already has a solution waiting to be found.

Problems are a natural part of life. There is no escaping them, and you should not expect to. Having problems to solve is how we grow as individuals.

When a problem arises, instead of complaining about it or ignoring it, brainstorm solutions.

Make efforts to solve the problem and move on. Optimists tend to be problem solvers. When you solve problems and negative situations instead of dwelling on them, you eliminate the negative energy that comes with them so that you are freer to have an optimistic outlook.

Forgive Yourself

We all make mistakes. Just as having problems to solve is a natural part of progressing through life, so is making mistakes. The best way to handle a mistake is to learn from it and avoid future mishaps.

Past mistakes are just that, in the past. But if you dwell on them, you cannot move on from the negative emotions and thoughts. This leads to pessimistic thinking.

Instead, learn from your mistakes and use them to make yourself a better person from the knowledge you've gained.

Make a conscious effort to move on and understand that your past does not define who you are, the choices you make in the present moment are a better indication of who you are as a person

Adopt a Healthy Lifestyle

Being physically fit and healthy leads to positive mental health and self-esteem.

Part of the reason for this is the neurotransmitters that are released into your body when you exercise. They not only improve your mood, but they also help you sleep better, improve learning and attention, boost your memory and brain activity, and block pain.

Eat healthy foods to fuel your body and brain with the nutrients you need to function at your best.

Adopt a healthy lifestyle further by eliminating harmful habits, such as smoking, excessive drinking, and insufficient sleep.

Serve Others

Service to others helps us forget our problems or at least put them into perspective.

When you are trying to help someone, you automatically try to be more optimistic and help them have a more positive outlook. As you encourage others, you will naturally cultivate optimism in yourself.

Service helps you feel better about yourself as well. It can help you have more realistic thinking patterns and improve your self-confidence. The positive energy you share with others will follow the law of compensation and spill over into creating positive energy in your own life.

Ask Why This Is Happening for You, Not to You

When you are faced with a difficult situation, you might do what many people do and ask why it is happening to you. However, you will learn how to be an optimist by asking why it is happening for you instead.

Changing this wording will help you change your perspective and see the blessings and benefits that can come out of challenging times instead of feeling like a victim.

It helps you feel in control, have an optimistic outlook, and change your thinking to focus on the opportunities and improvements the challenge can create.

Focus on What You Can Control

There are some things, however, that are out of our control. A sudden illness, death of a loved one, loss of a job, or natural disaster are not caused by us, yet they affect us.

Part of the power of realistic thinking is knowing what you can and cannot control and then focusing on what you can control.

Listing and putting your positive energy into the things you can control will help you feel less overwhelmed. For instance, you can control the steps you will take to find a new job, find a life coach or counselor that can help you go through the grieving process, and follow your physician's orders to relieve your symptoms.

One thing you can always control is how you react to negative situations and the way in which you think about them. Practice how to be an optimist by taking time to reflect instead of reacting. Make a conscious effort to choose positive thinking over negative thinking.

Laugh

You may have heard the saying laughter is the best medicine, and there is a lot of truth to that.

Humor is healing, both to our mental health and physical health. Laughing causes us to take in more oxygen, which relaxes us. It has a positive effect on how your heart functions, rids your body of cortisol, which is a stress hormone and activates the reward system in your brain.

Studies show that laughter also reduces pain, anxiety, and agitation. It improves how your brain works to make it easier to gain the skills to learn how to be an optimist. It has also been shown to improve the symptoms of medical conditions, including Parkinson's disease, rheumatoid arthritis, and schizophrenia.

Add humor into your daily life. This can start with a simple smile as well as include watching comical videos and movies, reading funny books, listening to humorous dialogues, and telling tasteful jokes.

Find humor in stressful moments as well. Without offending anyone or being disrespectful, laughing about a mishap or amid a stressful moment can put yourself and others at ease and help you have a positive outlook so you can work on the solution.

You Can Become More Optimistic

Now that you have these strategies on how to be optimistic to guide you, you can begin to put these ideas to work in your everyday life.

To further improve your ability to think positively, and be an optimist in every aspect of your life, use my personal development plan template. With this template, you can identify your areas of opportunity and improve your successes, while also learning to think ahead and evaluate your goals effectively.

Printed in Great Britain
by Amazon

26844014R00051